SANDTIQUITY

To Tara —

love yr.X (rated) student
Simo —

+ Kappy!
(you're my inspiration!)

TAPLINGER PUBLISHING COMPANY   NEW YORK

CONNIE SIMÓ, KAPPY WELLS, AND MALCOLM WELLS

SANDTIQUITY

This book is dedicated to our beach friends—
Shirley, Bobby, Daisy, Max, Dante, and Bambi

First Printing

Published in 1980 by
TAPLINGER PUBLISHING CO., INC.
New York, New York

Library of Congress Cataloging in Publication Data

Simó, Connie.
    Sandtiquity.

    1. Sand craft. 2. Sandcastles. 3. Sand sculpture.
I. Wells, Kappy, joint author. II. Wells, Malcolm,
joint author. III. Title.
TT865.S55   736'.9   78-20696
ISBN 0-8008-6989-3
ISBN 0-8008-6990-7 (pbk.)

CONTENTS

Introduction

One summer we found ourselves unaccountably tired of tanning, napping, snacking on gritty sandwiches, and supervising the kids' bucket sculpture. But we had also outgrown sand mermaids, and soupy, drip-constructed castles, and burying each other's legs. Our solution to summer boredom soon became a mania and never failed to draw curious crowds as we gained skill, confidence, and ingenuity in bringing vanished civilizations back to life.

We preserved our masterpieces in photographs before the tides and wind did their work, and these models took on the scale of the originals when the angle, lighting, and background were just right. We were surprised at the illusion of size and substance we created.

Some of the structures were grand to look at but took only minutes to build, while others were modest in size and deceptively tricky to get right. The only tools we needed were a straight, flat stick of wood and our eager hands. The damp sand did the rest, holding an extraordinary variety of shapes and angles. Some passersby insisted we must have used cardboard inserts to give us such crisp, solid-looking edges, but we claimed that the structures were buried there—we had simply brushed away the sand.

The wind-blurred results of one of our first attempts.

7

We had a wealth of building styles to draw from, stretching back five thousand years. Man's earliest buildings depended on the force of gravity, stone upon stone, more than any internal framework to keep them standing, so they're particularly well suited to reproduction in sand. Like all self-respecting architects, we borrowed ideas from different eras and far-flung continents, gaining a knowledgeable respect for our ancient colleagues along the way. We also began to view the buildings around us in a new way, almost as sculpture, noting the play of light and shadow and wondering how they would look in sand.

Deir El Bahari. Our view is from below.

We came to welcome the gentle aging effects of the wind and the minor avalanches that made ruins of our work, just as the elements had created the ruins that inspired us. It was as if time had shrunk along with physical dimension, and we watched like lazy gods as the sun went down.

A ziggurat, an ancient Persian temple on a man-made hill.

CHAPTER ONE

Formal Structures

The straightedges we used were always found things, a piece of broken dune fencing, a scrap of shingle, anything that had a flat side for tamping surfaces and a true edge for slicing and shaping. After a few days of use, the anonymous bits of wood seemed to fit our hands like cherished old tools, and we were not amused when somebody's dog tried to make off with a favorite stick.

The sand we worked with varied from one site to another, but as long as it was damp and free of seaweed, shells, and pebbles, it performed admirably. Damp sand will stand at a much steeper angle than dry, and it can even be made to hold a vertical surface or slight overhang without collapsing. At about fifteen feet from the water's edge, the sand was always perfect for molding—neither too soupy nor too dry—but after a day of rain we were free to build anywhere and our shapes held beautifully.

Water is the mortar that holds our structures together. After a short exposure to the sun, the surfaces will look dry, but the sand inside remains moist for hours. Careful packing of the surfaces not only gives the objects a finished, solid look, but prevents evaporation of the vital moisture.

We soon learned that the ultimate success of a structure depended on the care we took to get our corners sharp and true and our surfaces smooth and compact. Without that care, the buildings looked unconvincing, more like crumbly cookies than impressive tombs and temples. But a real masterwork was admired by everyone who passed. Half the fun was moving off down the beach and watching our pieces attract and astound.

A fantasy structure—call it a corduroy road on a dome.

One of our early landscapes—a strange melange of Egypt and South America.

An abstract formation took on a shell-like quality.

One of our earlier efforts was the elegant Egyptian pyramid. These royal tombs were actually as tall as five hundred feet, covering thirteen acres, but our small version captured the feeling of mass and awed bathers and joggers with its mystery.

Simple shapes like this one are not the easiest to construct, but mastering these crisp corners and smooth faces gave us the skill we needed to make any other sand construction look convincing, solid, and larger than life.

The basic pyramid is built on a square base, and marking out the square before carving the sides helped us find the right proportions.

First we brush away the dry surface sand and heap up the damp sand into a mound half again as high as the finished size.

Then we pat it into a rough shape, compacting the sand as we work.

We begin to carve the sides with our straightedge. A bold, confident stroke works best.

We go over each face several times, packing the sand tighter with the flat side of our stick to give it that look of solid magnificence.

We use the shadow from our straightedge
to check the flatness of a surface.

The crooked shadow tells us we
sliced unevenly.

The power of these structures cannot be
overstated, crumbly sand though they may be.

We ran a ramp down one side of our pyramid and then gave it some dimension as it meandered along the beach. The regular indentations seemed like the tracks of a mighty machine, emphasized by bright sunlight and shadow. We watched the shadows in all the work we did. They showed up every flaw and kept our carving regular and smooth.

Here we started with a simple pyramid and carved further, lopping off the top and re-shaping the sides. The cuts took less than a minute, then we stood back and admired the sun's effect. A bird's-eye view revealed a striking pinwheel.

This twisted pyramid is also carved on a square base. We patted it into the general shape we wanted, then sliced with the stick. We treated the fragile corners gently, holding the flat of the wood against the surface and tapping it with a finger. The circular base helped anchor it to the rest of the landscape.

Once the surfaces were smooth and flat, corners sharp, we gave the pyramid added authenticity and scale by pushing faint horizontal dents into the faces. It looks as if it were built up of great dressed stones when done right. Practice gave us a lighter touch—the slightest indentation catches the light when surfaces are even.

In another variation we added ramps and used burnt matches to represent people, making the pyramid look even more huge. The bird tracks were our undoing.

Here, addition of small, low buildings connected by a causeway to a giant pyramid begins to suggest a great tomb complex, such as the one found at Giza. Add some smaller pyramids and temples of other shapes and you'll have no trouble imagining a royal Egyptian buried beneath millions of tons of rock.

When we began this structure it was only a stepped round thing, but our spectators and critics insisted it was a Greek amphitheater, and who were we to argue? We didn't faithfully follow the ancient design but tried to imagine tiny actors and spectators in scale and finished our theater to suit that purpose.

Any time you want to make a perfect semi-circle, hold your stick with your arm quite stiff and then swing from your elbow for a small semicircle and from your shoulder for a larger one.

As shown in the pictures on this page, we started with a gently sloping sand hill and patted a rough semicircle. Then, swinging from the shoulder, we carved our first step and smoothed and packed below the first tier. In carving the next step, we used the top edge of the stick to measure the depth. Pressing against the top step gave us a sharp edge and, again, we packed the sand below so the steps would remain firm.

Far upper left: we cut the fourth step.

Far lower left: a close-up of the packing process. Every surface needs this going over to hold the sand.

Upper left: we give a lot of attention to the corners, and if we happen to crumble one in our enthusiasm, we simply heap on more damp sand and recarve.

Lower left: actors enter here. We finish everything in arm's reach as we move along.

When the surfaces were tightly packed and clean, the shadows they created were striking. Upside down the photographs fool the eye, turning bowl shapes into mounds, because we read shadows as falling *down* from an object with the light source above it. Flipping through this book upside down reveals stranger shapes than we ever dreamed of.

This stepped pyramid is based on a variety found throughout Central America. The stairs were on one or more faces and the priests would climb them to the level top where they performed sacrifices. Our version seemed to possess a mysterious power which drew an audience from all over the beach.

Far upper left: we start with a basic pyramid, level the top, and square it.

Far lower left: we inscribe the sides of the ramp.

Upper left: we indent the ramp using the width of our stick.

Lower left: we shave away some sand on either side and smooth the raised part.

Far upper left: using the end of the stick, we push in little steps.

Far lower left: we use the width of the stick to measure the steps and press them flat.

Upper left: it takes a sharp eye to keep the steps horizontal on a sloping beach.

Lower left: the front steps are last. We have to make minor adjustments to line them up on either side of the ramp.

The audience gathered around and stared
as if waiting for the priest to arrive and the
ceremony to begin. And we weren't the
only ones taking pictures. Did you realize
the structure was quite this small?

The ziggurat was an artificial mountain built high above the plains to support a sacred shrine. The shrine, reaching up to the heavens, was meant to attract a visitation of the deity. Ruins of more than thirty ziggurats still exist in the Middle East. Our version is modeled after the ruins at Ur, and, to the best of our knowledge, it attracted no gods but many, many pilgrims in bathing suits.

We didn't finish this building in the usual smooth, even way because it looked like a creditable ruin in its rough state. The condition of the sand reminded us of ancient bricks, so we took it one step further and experimented with a texture on the walls.

We cleared some space directly around it and roughed up the sand beyond that to give the illusion that a great hunk of land had been cleared before building began. Then we stuck our chins in the sand and gazed in awe at our creation.

The picture on the opposite page shows the details of the ziggurat.

We start with a damp mound almost twice the size of the finished structure, pack it, and rough in the temple on top.

We work quickly down the mountain, cutting ledges and leaving ramps to connect the levels.

Halfway up the slope we cut a small tower and top it with a domed cap.

We carve out an impressive front, using an old ruler this time.

We never felt that a structure was truly finished until we had provided it with some sort of base. The simplest base is an area of smoothed sand around a structure where it can sit like an actor on an empty stage, gathering all attention to itself. This worked best for our plainer, monumental forms, while the busier plazas lent a look of utility to houses, villages, and abstract works. Architects and emperors alike have long recognized the importance of creating appropriate settings.

"But where are the footprints?" everyone asks. Well, we wear skis all day. And back away from our work, smoothing the sand as we go.

A broad base is like the velvet rope in a museum —it keeps the spectators a respectful distance away.

We take the natural slope of the beach, define it with smooth planes, and add some mysterious structures. The untouched areas take on their own importance in an abstract like this.

A road approaches the temple up several levels, reminding us of the stately avenues leading to the Washington Monument and L'Arc de Triomphe. Why didn't we try *those* in sand?

These triangular terraces formed a backdrop for a landscape.

CHAPTER TWO

Simple Structures and Groupings

Our loaves are built one at a time, no preplanning necessary. After the first is heaped up and shaped, we make a mound next door and shape again, then level the ground.

These barrel-vaulted dwellings are modeled after a type that originated in ancient Greece, and it was easy to imagine them serenely facing the Aegean Sea. Traditionally, each little loaf was a single room and there were no interior connections between them. Since ours was built on a steep hillside, we made it a split-level, and we improvised with windows and ridges along the roofs. After all, we are architects, not drudges.

Additions to the family? Add more rooms.

There was a lot of satisfaction in building smaller structures. They had a different but powerful appeal, perhaps because their scale was immediately apparent. Our ever-changing audience seemed to think that gnomes lived in them. One young fellow even tried to peer through the doorway.

Domed houses like this one were built in the Middle East centuries ago. They had thick, windowless walls and inset doorways to keep out the fierce desert heat.

We add the dome to the flattened roof and shape it firmly before slicing away the walls. The small ledge at the entrance gives a touch of realism.

Sharp angles and planes of light and shadow give our little house substance. A desert family can move right in.

The caravanserai were desert inns found everywhere in the Middle East, often spaced a day's journey apart. The sail-vaulted roofs give an inkling of what the interior space would be like, a dark and airy haven in the scorching desert. This is only one of many roof forms that man has drawn from nature.

Above: as the sun set on our little model, we thought we spotted a camel on the horizon. But then again, it might just have been the neighbor's dog.

Right: we roughly cut the walls from a heap of sand and form the top into irregular domes, supporting the wall with one hand. We quickly learn how hard we can pat without causing a collapse.

Far right: a small mound of sand added to the front wall is cut into buttresses.

What looks like a tiny modern house is actually an early tomb from Mesopotamia. It is just one step removed from the simple grave mound, but its basic features were used in tomb design for the next two thousand years. The domed burial chamber was meant to represent the cosmos and in later versions grew into a taller, beehive shape, then into a cone, and eventually into the pyramid. The long passageway led from this life to the afterlife.

Left: we pat as smooth a hemisphere as we can, using the sunlight and shadows to find irregularities, then add the general shape of the passage.

Upper left: we slice the curved roof and clear away the excess sand.

Above: we try to keep the base of the dome a neat circle.

Upper right: the handle of a picnic spoon is our tool for inscribing the structural lines.

As beginners we were obsessed with the size and scope of single structures, but we soon discovered the thrill of ranging over wide areas, transforming the landscape with our works. We let the existing contours of the beach influence us in designing the spaces between our structures and left natural areas to contrast with our carved planes and shapes. As we created, we tried to imagine the flow of activities that might take place on our landscapes— in miniature, of course!

Below left: we like to combine simple shapes, loosely based on ancient ones, in brand-new ways, with only inspiration to guide us.

Left: the road is taking over in this landscape, winding its way *over* the forms it was supposed to connect. Well, we can't be purists every day.

Below: sometimes we find we are more interested in in-betweens than in structures. Roads begin to take on solid form and waves are appearing in our planes!

Here's a landscape that never got off the ground. We were in a mood to carve but not to heap. The result is this geometric design with a high-tech look. Think of it as a subterranean construction and imagine the rest.

The repetition of a simple shape enhances its mysterious presence, as with these truncated pyramids. If one is important, three are three times that.

Cultures meet and mingle on our stretch of beach. A landscape is created here more by nearness than design.

This undecided roadway was dragged with the wide end of a stick. A little pressure pushed up the sides along the way.

CHAPTER THREE

Complexes

The practice of burrowing into already-formed structures was common all over the ancient world. Our adaptation was based on the Anatolian hill villages, where conical volcanic formations were eroded by wind and weather and the natural caves were carved out further by the ancients and used as dwellings. We should admit that our little hills did not occur naturally on the beach—we heaped and packed them.

Above right: rough textures too are achieved with the straightedge stick.

Right: our doorways are poked in with a handy barrette. All that's missing are the rope ladders.

Above far right: the next hill is formed and packed.

Far right: our little village provided one of our most dramatic sunsets.

Some ancient Egyptian tombs were carved into the ground and their interiors were traditionally elaborate. But we concerned ourselves with the false doorway that was believed to be the passageway to the afterlife and was decorated in bas-relief.

Our tomb entrance and the plaza before it were cut into an existing slope on the beach. The doorway was tightly packed and the portrait of the pharaoh was produced by trial and error, which is no trouble at all in sand carving, luckily. Our results were surprisingly effective. We left the sand rough around the excavation for realism.

This whole project was a race against the tide.

The tide won.

Our walled city was really just a rough
sketch of a town, an impression built of
many details. The varying height of the wall
and of the buildings within suggested a
natural topography of the land. Steps and
stairways were provided to connect the
levels. A massive retaining wall behind the
complex was all that remained of the
original site.

The wall is first cut and formed around a shapeless mound. Then we stamp out the town with a new tool, a small square block nailed to a straightedge. We press lightly for a roof top, harder for a courtyard, twirl it for circles, angle it, and make steps with it.

The massive wall not only makes our town invincible, but gives it a satisfying unity. It is entirely self-contained, a democratic city-state, we like to think.

Above: our fort is a haven in this rugged wilderness.

The interior ramp and tiny doorways are the sort of details that give scale to any construction and add to the illusion.

Our version of a pentagon fort has a lethal point radiating out from each side. It's a made-up design, but leaves no doubt as to its function. We're on the defensive here, secure against any enemy attack—except the dreaded beach ball.

Another way we connected structures and created complexes was by carving out steps and terraces. These differ from bases and plazas mostly in their imagined function. Often, a base became a plaza when it stretched out before some building or monument, and steps grew broader and broader until they were terraces. They all tended to flow together and follow the lay of the beach when inspiration was upon us. When we were done, the eye played tricks, picking out what seemed to be a foot-sized step and enlarging everything around that accordingly. Are these steps a man would walk up, or sit on, or scale?

Whatever scale we chose to work in, the effects we achieved were well beyond the actual size of our creations. It was always a surprise to smooth off a last plain, lay our stick aside, sink down on the sand, and gaze up at a temple or cliff face or monument.

Here we had little height, so we played with the inner angles.

Right: sometimes we placed angle on angle.

Far right: where else can you build a grand staircase in minutes?

Below: from some views these graded terraces echo the shape of the flat-topped pyramid behind.

Then came the day when we didn't feel geometrical at all and our terraces undulated along the sloping sand with no plan other than our own amusement and satisfaction.

Here's another variation—ramps, stairways without steps. These have a very clean, solid look, more like modern poured concrete than ancient ruins. Or sand.

On the opposite page: these abstract fancies,
too, drew the attention of every passerby. What
could be more appropriate than waves on the
beach?

Our groundworks cover a lot of area in a very
short time and sharpen up our carving and
packing skills. It gives a feeling of real power to
transform a strip of beach this way.

CHAPTER FOUR

Monumentality

High up in the Andes are the ruins of
Machu Picchu, a sort of vast theater-in-the-
round that held as many as sixty thousand
people. We can only guess at the spec-
tacles that took place there and marvel
at the engineering feat of the ancient Incas.
The actual tiers are each six feet high and
twenty-three feet deep, carved right out of
the mountain. These were monumental
works, and our little sand model captured
their scale admirably.

**Above: even with the ocean in the background
it's hard to tell the size of our Machu Picchu.**

**Left: judge by the piece of snow fencing—it's
that small!**

A view from inside. We started with two footprint-shaped depressions and carved the tiers from the top down, carefully clearing out the excess sand at each level.

Each step and tier is as high as the width of our stick. The shadows would have told on us if there was unevenness there. We also made sure to keep all our planes horizontal. The success of a piece, its power to convince and surprise, depends on details like these.

The sculptor is backing down through the valley, touching up along her way. We have already made sand look like bricks and concrete and dressed stone. Now we're shaping it into hillsides.

The vertical face of the dam was packed tightly and smoothly to give it a man-made look to contrast with the rougher surroundings.

We arrived at the beach one day full of enough energy and ambition to move the earth. We constructed this dam instead. It's another sort of monumental design that gained its credibility through our molding of the ravines and valley behind it, and the great basin that suggested a thunderous flow of water pounding away at it for ages and ages. The afternoon sun lent a dramatic effect and convinced us of our dam's solidity.

The wall is built up by packing a small mound of damp sand on the top of the edge of the arc and carving it into a raised rim.

The water level is carefully graded.

On the opposite page: the two watch towers were also built from a small heap of sand and then packed and cut away.

The Buddha figure is formed with the usual straightedge, but it's used with a rolling motion of the flat side, cutting, packing, and shaping at the same time. The fleshy, almost obscene lump manages to convince us of its serenity as it sits in a place of honor.

This was a fifteen-minute project, a race against the tide, which was lapping at our steps. Then we let the ocean wash the great Buddha away.

The scalloped steps were cut quickly by eye. After the first wave almost reached the Buddha, the steps begin to crumble.

Another try at modeling, this sphinx reminded us of nothing so much as a long-earred puppy dog. But when the light was right, we flopped down on our bellies and thought it looked rather profound.

"It's exactly like a real sphinx," our audience said. We didn't give them an argument.

For our version of the Great Wall of China, we made a mound that snaked along the beach following miniature hills and valleys. We added turrets of our own design and the roadway on top was inscribed with a popsicle stick.

We packed the walls in such a way that the vertical dents suggested masonry.

These structures—Deir el Bahari and Giza— were modeled after two of the great mortuary temples of ancient Egypt. The tomb was regarded by the Egyptians as the permanent home of the spirit, and so great was its importance that little attention was spared to other problems in architecture. Deir el Bahari, on the right, was originally carved out of a cliff face. We shaped a rugged landscape behind our version to suggest a similar engineering feat.

The broad forecourt and gently sloping ramp gives this temple a serene and solemn aspect. We built our ramps a bit high, then pressed the stick down the center to give us side railings.

The small details—doors, roof bands, textures —add to the monumentality and keep a simple structure from looking simpleminded.

The dawn of history or sunset at the beach?

On the opposite page: besides helping us keep edges and planes straight and smooth, bright sunlight and shadow lent a look of massiveness to our sand-works that a gray day couldn't.

This gateway ended up looking surprisingly solid. The mound we start from is quite rough, but notice the evenness and sharp detail on the part we have formed.

Our finishing of the courtyard inside
is as important as the gate itself in
achieving an effect.

How many soldiers could march abreast
through this gate?

We caught it on film just a moment before the
sun went down, the most dramatic time of day.

We didn't always restrict ourselves to geometrical forms, but even our flights of fancy received crisp edges. This shell-like formation seems to rise in gentle curves and then become subterranean. Above, the looping lines repeat the shell motif. And on the right, it emerges looking like the twisted waves of a riptide or possibly a congregation of mollusks. On the upper right there is a detail showing the pattern of sunlight and shadow.

Which civilization built *this* casual thing? It looks like a cartoon observatory.

From a respectful angle, with plenty of shadow, it becomes a venerable ruin.

The abstract on the opposite page was carved along a tide shelf and so it naturally followed the horizontal. The shadows make it stand out in bold relief.

CHAPTER FIVE

The Lay of the Land

Along the beach you will find all sorts of mounds and tidal benches and strange configurations—sometimes the remnants of the play of others—which make splendid springboards for a little carving and readapting of your own.

This wall of sand was just waiting for people with imagination to come and claim it. We sketched in a roadway and a few mysterious facades and it became a Tibetan monastery. Then the tide claimed it.

The lofty monastery takes on a mysterious majesty when photographed from below.

On the opposite page: starting with a simple heap of sand, we sculpted the ridge, flattened it, added tiny cliff faces, and it became a mesa.

Remember Devil's Tower from *Close Encounters of the Third Kind?* We thought we might lure a tiny UFO with this replica. It took only a few minutes to shape the tower top, rocking the edge of our stick against it to give it texture.

This inspiring heap was found at the base of a lifeguard's chair. We went to work with our straightedges and turned it into a primitive mountainside village, making it up as we went along. By the time we were through, it was covered with dwellings and storehouses, shrines, corridors, and steps in every direction. There were terraces all down the front, and most of the windows and doorways faced out to sea, the better to watch for the approaching storm.

We decided to beat the weather and destroy it ourselves. It took real daring to cartwheel down those solid-looking steps.

It took an afternoon to build and five minutes of great fun to demolish.

A small depression got us started here. We carved it into a deeper heart shape, smoothed the surrounding sand, and cut channels until the pattern suggested itself.

When we stood back, we couldn't decide whether it was a cloverleaf road system or a landing field for extraterrestrials.

Is there a more relaxing way to spend time at the beach than smoothing and shaping?

Faint marks left over from some sort of beach game were the start of this random pattern.

Another view of it when we added some weird pyramids lower on the beach. They look more like semi-collapsed tents or limpet shells.

We revisited a day-old site and found some tempting remains. Before we knew it, we had our sticks out, patterning in swirls like tank tracks.

This appeared to be the leavings of a novice builder when we stumbled on it, a U-shaped wall formed only by bare hands. We took our straight sticks to it and shaped it up.

Another race against the tide, with the inevitable result.

This sand wall had some vertical grooves. We packed it tighter and carved a very shallow cave and more vertical and horizontal details and had a perfect spot for a Pueblo village.

CHAPTER SIX

Time and Tide

Nothing we built was beyond the reach of wind or tide, nor was it meant to be. It was exciting to watch an especially powerful wave crash down upon a temple or village and wipe it out, while the slower erosion of the wind set us to daydreaming—the structures fall to ruin on a tiny scale much the way ancient stones and bricks crumble over the course of centuries. The speeded-up, natural weathering often makes a structure more impressive than it was in its first pristine minutes of completion.

This unassuming little dome was an experiment. We patted it as smooth as could be and stood back to watch the wind do its work. Within an hour it had returned to its elements.

The waves swept in and enveloped our crazy dome following the swirls we had cut ourselves.

The U-shaped mound is almost as we found it.

The first wave batters one of our more ambitious ramps.

Nature makes its additions to our carefully worked designs. New textures appear, bits of flotsam decorate our once-smooth planes, ravines are cut wider and deeper.

It made us wistful to come back to a piece after the wind had its way. The sharp clean edges are gone, and sand has sifted into the corners. We hardly recognize the work of our own hands.

The next day we returned and found the previous evening's activities detailed across our work, dog tracks, bird and human footprints, but still there was a measure of respect. One doesn't lightly destroy a temple.

The ramp above, once high on the beach, now leads directly to the sea.

The waves surround our odd, turret-like pyramid.

A single pyramid is isolated on a sand flat.

The lacy foam reaches out for a terrace-pool complex.

Nature abhors a sharp plane. As the water swirls over the lower terrace it smooths the contours into gentle hills.

With the next wave, the rectangular reflecting pool will be only an oval depression. Soon all this will be sea-washed beach—virgin land for tomorrow's builder.

The surf approaches our pyramid complex.

Now the pyramid is assaulted...

...and once conquered by a wave, it can't last long.

"Thus," said Henry Thoreau, "all work passes
out of the hands of the architect into the
hands of nature, to be perfected."